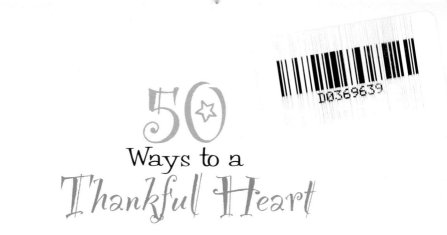

50 Ways to a
Thankful Heart

Jane C. Jarrell
Artwork by Lila Rose Kennedy

HARVEST HOUSE PUBLISHERS
EUGENE, OR

Dedicated to: Chelsey Elizabeth Cabaniss

50 Ways to a Thankful Heart

Text Copyright © 2000 by Jane C. Jarrell
Published by Harvest House Publishers
Eugene, Oregon 97402

ISBN 0-7369-0219-8

Artwork designs are reproduced under license from © Arts Uniq'®, Inc., Cookeville, TN and may not be reproduced without permission. For information regarding art prints featured in this book please contact:

> Arts Uniq'
> P. O. Box 3085
> Cookeville, TN 38502
> 800-223-5020

Design and production by Garborg Design Works, Minneapolis, Minnesota

Scriptures quotations are taken from The Promise™ copyright © 1995, Thomas Nelson, Inc.; from the Holy Bible, New International Version®, Copyright © 1973, 1978, 1984 by the International Bible Society. Used by permission of Zondervan Publishing House; and from the New American Standard Bible, © 1960, 1962, 1963, 1968, 1971, 1972, 1973, 1975, 1977 by The Lockman Foundation. Used by permission.

Printed in China.

00 01 02 03 04 05 06 07 08 09 /PP/ 10 9 8 7 6 5 4 3 2 1

A thankful heart experiences sunshine even on the darkest days.
AUTHOR UNKNOWN

Gratitude is when your heart smiles. Thankful hearts smile a lot. Puppies and rainbows and walking in puddles after the rain are just some of the little things we can thank God for. You will love the 50 special things listed here that make life happy. But besides just *what* to be thankful for, you will also find sections that help you see *who* you can be thankful for, simple gift ideas for *how* to show thankfulness, and even one to explain how Mommy is thankful. It's good for Mommy to have a happy heart too!

Gratitude is not only the greatest of virtues, but the parent of all others.
CICERO

WHAT ARE YOU THANKFUL FOR?

*"I will bless them...I will send down showers in season;
there will be showers of blessing."*
THE BOOK OF EZEKIEL

Showers of blessings can be a lot like raindrops; they're sometimes hard to see. You know only by the freshness in the air and the bright colors in the garden that the showers have come as blessings.

What are you thankful for? How long has it been since you stopped to think about God's blessings to you?

My heart is thankful for...

Walking in puddles after a rain.

Petting my pets little head.

$\mathcal{P}$icking fresh flowers and dandelions
and taking them to Mom.

$\mathcal{C}$ounting
the
shining
stars.

The glow in my room when the sun goes down.

The way my little doll looks.

7

Feeling really good about making
the right choice.

Being surprised by
a rainbow.

Getting enough allowance to go Christmas shopping.

Taking a walk to find out how many different bugs and leaves I can find.

Going to a barber shop and being pleased
with what I see in the mirror.

Being thankful for band-aids
after I fall down.

The first time I played a song on the piano,
even with just one hand.

Having my favorite foods at Thanksgiving dinner.

Remembering what I wanted when I went to talk to my teacher.

Learning to love crunchy vegetables just because they are good for me.

You're Our HERO!

17 Opening my Valentines.

18 Dressing up for church.

Running through the sprinkler
on the way to the
ice cream truck.

Having an extra
quarter to get a
treat at the store.

Homemade banana ice cream with hot fudge sauce.

Finding my favorite book at the library.

Finding tadpoles in the creek beds.

Being able to say my ABCs.

A new baby in our home.

My
favorite
toy
train.

My first ride on the school bus.

My favorite teacher's smile.

Chocolate-dipped
pretzel sticks.

My BIG box of dress up clothes.

My Easter basket full of
delicious candies.

A trip to the Farmers Market to
choose the best berries for our pie.

Really funny movies, watched with popcorn and M&Ms.

Planting colorful flowers in the front porch pots.

Swinging as high as I can on my backyard swing.

Taking a break at the mall for a big, warm chocolate chip cookie.

Catching lightning bugs
on a warm summer night.

Jumping in a
swimming pool after
a hot game of baseball.

Hot chocolate after a great snowball fight.

Riding down the hill on the sled with my dad.

$\mathcal{L}$earning to ride a bike
without training wheels.

$\mathcal{S}$itting on the back porch
and blowing bubbles.

Heart-shaped
suckers with
sprinkles.

My first
ballet recital
outfit.

My first goal in soccer.

45

Hot pizza delivered to our doorstep.

46

GIFT CERTIFICATE

My first box of paper dolls.

Doing a sack race with my best friend.

The way the house smells
when bread is baking.

Jumping off the diving board
for the first time.

WHO ARE YOU THANKFUL FOR?

God is who you can be most thankful for. He loves you when you are happy and He loves you when you are sad. Gods love is always here for you and that should make you glad! It is also good to be thankful for the different people in your life...parents, grandparents, aunts, uncles, and friends. Life is so much brighter when you share love and happy feelings with the people all around you.

Who are the people who make the world a better place for you?

My mommy, who smiles at me so sweetly and hugs me so warmly when I wake up from a nap.

My grandmom, who plays the piano and sings with me, even when I make up the songs.

My grandpa, who takes me out to help him feed his little stray cat friends.

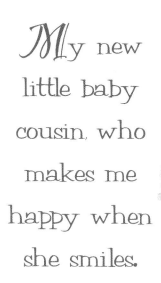

My new
little baby
cousin, who
makes me
happy when
she smiles.

B·A·B·Y

33

My grandmother, who takes me swimming and holds me tight when I get a little frightened of the water.

My auntie, who takes me to our special breakfast place and lets me eat jelly out of the little packages.

My big cousin, who helps me through the tall scary tunnels at the hamburger place.

My granddad, who lets me help him water the flower garden and doesn't mind if I get wet too.

My special little neighbor friend, who catches lightning bugs with me on warm spring evenings.

My aunt and uncle, who bring little surprises for no other reason than because it makes me happy inside.

My daddy, who takes me to the mall to watch the ice skaters and always gets me a great candy treat.

My mommy and daddy, all the time but especially at bedtime, who read to me and listen to me say my prayers.

HOW DO YOU SHOW THANKFULNESS?

To show someone a big thank you makes that person feel good. Do something to make a special person happy; maybe a little gift or a big hug. Doing something nice for someone can really make your heart smile. Try a BIG smile, a sweet little note, or a special box of candy. Always look for ways to show others that you love them. This special attitude of gratitude will make your heart grow and grow.

Every good gift and every
perfect gift is from above,
coming down from the Father.
THE BOOK OF JAMES

How can you show someone special you're thankful for them?

A small bouquet of fresh cut flowers in a jelly jar with a colorful bow tied around the top to give to Mom on May Day.

Bubble bath and a
    scented votive candle
for my big sister.

    A brightly colored
        notebook with
    special stickers for
    my favorite teacher.

A little glass heart paper weight for
daddy to use in his office.

A special treat from my favorite
bakery wrapped in a big bow for
the neighbor next door.

A gift certificate for a great kids' magazine like Barney, Sesame Street, or Crayola Kids for my favorite cousin.

A beach towel and suntan lotion for my best aunt.

SPF 20

A fancy key chain
for Mommy's keys.

A dress up outfit of a storybook
character for my brother.

A lip pencil and matching lip color in the season's newest shade for my favorite babysitter.

A "wait watchers" bag filled with crayons and activity books for my little sister.

45

A pretty bow with matching ankle socks for my best friend.

A pretty calendar for the new year for my ballet teacher.

A pretty coffee mug filled with flavored cocoa and a bag of mini marshmallows for my Sunday school teacher.

A jar of homemade preserves for my soccer coach.

A personalized placemat for my terrific uncle.

Some prepared cookie dough with a small bag of cookie cutters for my Brownie troop leader.

A little picture frame with
dried flowers glued around
the edges for grandma.

A fun computer program
for my big brother.

A small picture album filled with pictures from a special event, like a birthday, holiday, or a trip to the museum, for Papa and Nana.

A box of chocolate candy for my piano teacher.

A series of little books about my special friend's favorite subject.

A terra cotta pot filled with packages
of flower seeds to plant
in the window of my
cousin's fort.

ZINNIA

A package of stick-on earrings
for special dress-up occasions for
the little girl down the street.

Three colors of Play-Doh
and cookie cutters for my little brother.

MOMMY IS THANKFUL FOR...

Her children rise up and bless her.
THE BOOK OF PROVERBS

*M*ommies are thankful for so many things. A Mommy is grateful when she hears little feet pitter-pattering down a hardwood hallway on the way for the first morning hug. A Mommy is grateful when she sees her child offer comfort to another child that is unhappy. A Mommy is grateful when just two bites of broccoli are eaten. A Mommy is grateful when the very first ballet recital has been performed. A Mommy is grateful when the doctor gives an all clear signal after a nasty ear infection. A Mommy is grateful when the swimming lessons go smoothly.

What are some things you can do to help Mommy have an attitude of gratitude?

Getting the diapers and bottle to help Mom with the new baby.

Handing Daddy the remote.

Bringing in the mail
from the mail box.

Being careful with
my new books.

Taking care of
my toys.

Doing what my parents ask the first time.

Speaking kind words as often as I can.

Threading the needle
for my grandmother.

Saying "I love you" to Mom or Dad before I hang up the phone.

Feeding my neighbors' pets
while they are away.

Bear with Balloons

A Airplane B C Carrot

Helping my younger brother
or sister learn their letters.

Tucking a little "love note" in Daddy's brief case.

Giving my parents a great big hug
when they return home.

Count Your Blessings

Count your blessings, name them one by one,
Count your blessings, see what God hath done!
Count your blessings, name them one by one,
And it will surprise you what the Lord hath done.

JOHNSON OATMAN, JR.